EGYPT
the people

Arlene Moscovitch

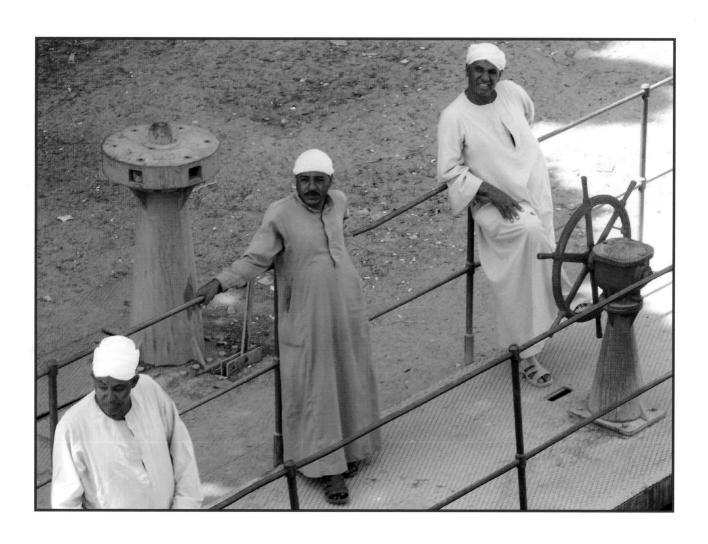

A Bobbie Kalman Book

The Lands, Peoples, and Cultures Series

Crabtree Publishing Company
www.crabtreebooks.com

The Lands, Peoples, and Cultures Series

Created by Bobbie Kalman

Coordinating editor
Ellen Rodger
Proofreader: Adrianna Morganelli
Project development
First Folio Resource Group, Inc.
   Pauline Beggs
   Tom Dart
   Kathryn Lane
   Debbie Smith
   Joyce Funamoto
   Robyn Craig
Design
David Vereschagin/Quadrat Communications

Revisions and updates
Plan B Book Packagers
Redbud Editorial

Special thanks to
Prof. Dr. Ahmed ElSherbini, Consul, Bureau
of Cultural and Education Affairs of Egypt;
Dr. N. B. Millet, Senior Curator, Egyptian Section,
Royal Ontario Museum; Magda Mousa, Principal,
MISR Language School

Photographs
Archive/Photo Researchers: p. 7 (top left);
Bill Bachmann/Bruce Coleman, Inc.: cover;
Corbis/Bettmann: p. 9 (bottom); Corbis/Bettmann-
UPI: p. 9 (top); Corbis/Marc Garanger: p. 22
(bottom); Marc Crabtree: p. 4 (bottom), p. 5,
p. 10 (left), p. 11 (top), p. 12, p. 13, p. 15 (bottom), p. 19 (bottom),
p. 21 (left), p. 25 (bottom), pp. 26–28 (all), p. 29 (top and bottom
left), p. 31 (bottom); Peter Crabtree: p. 7 (right), p. 23 (top); Milos
Gacanovic/Shutterstock, Inc.: p. 16 (top); Sylvain Grandadam/
Photo Researchers: p. 18; Imapress/Archive Photos: p. 11 (bottom);
André Klaassen/Shutterstock, Inc.: p. 16 (bottom); Mehmet Fatih
Kocyildir/Shutterstock, Inc.: p. 4; Vladimir Korostyshevskiy/
Shutterstock, Inc.: p. 1, p. 15 (top), p. 20; Richard T. Nowitz: p. 6
(bottom), p. 8 (both), p. 10 (right), p. 17 (middle), p. 21 (right), p. 22
(top), p. 23 (bottom), p. 24 (both), p. 30 (both); C. Osborne/Photo
Researchers: p. 31 (top);Pierdelune/Shutterstock, Inc.: p. 14; Carl
Purcell: p. 15 (middle); Scala/Art Resource, NY: p. 6 (top); SEF/
Art Resource, NY: p. 3; Werner Forman/Art Resource, NY: p. 7
(bottom left); Laura Zito/Photo Researchers: p. 17 (top and bottom),
p. 29 (bottom right)
Every effort has been made to obtain the appropriate credit and full
copyright clearance for all images in this book. Any oversites, despite
Crabtree's greatest precautions, will be corrected in future editions.

Illustrations
William Kimber. Male and female hieroglyphs appear at the head of
each section. The Great Sphinx is shown on the back cover.

Cover
Many people in Egypt make their living from tourism, one of the
country's biggest industries. This young Egyptian woman is selling
pottery in the local market.

Title page
Egyptian men dressed in lightweight cotton *galabyas*, the traditional
clothing worn by both men and women.

Library and Archives Canada Cataloguing in Publication

Moscovitch, Arlene, 1946-
   Egypt : the people / Arlene Moscovitch.

(Lands, peoples, and cultures series)
Includes index.
ISBN 978-0-7787-9306-9 (bound)
ISBN 978-0-7787-9674-9 (pbk.)

   1. Egypt--Social conditions--Juvenile literature. I. Title.
II. Series.

HN786.A8M67 2007   j962   C2007-905715-2

Library of Congress Cataloging-in-Publication Data

Moscovitch, Arlene, 1946-
   Egypt the people / Arlene Moscovitch.
      p. cm. -- (Lands, peoples, and cultures)
   Includes index.
   ISBN-13: 978-0-7787-9306-9 (rlb)
   ISBN-10: 0-7787-9306-0 (rlb)
   ISBN-13: 978-0-7787-9674-9 (pb)
   ISBN-10: 0-7787-9674-4 (pb)
   1. Egypt--Social life and customs--Juvenile literature. I. Title.
DT107.826.M67 2007
962--dc22
                                                        2007037300

Crabtree Publishing Company

www.crabtreebooks.com   1-800-387-7650

Printed in the USA/122015/CG20151105

Published in Canada
Crabtree Publishing
616 Welland Ave.
St. Catharines, Ontario
L2M 5V6

Published in the United States
Crabtree Publishing
PMB 59051
350 Fifth Avenue, 59th Floor
New York, New York 10118

Published in the United Kingdom
Crabtree Publishing
Maritime House
Basin Road North, Hove
BN41 1WR

Published in Australia
Crabtree Publishing
3 Charles Street
Coburg North
VIC 3058

Contents

Today's Egyptians live in a land that has the longest recorded history of any country in the world. Their way of life, religion, clothing, homes, and food have all been influenced by the many different peoples who have lived in Egypt over thousands of years and by the geography of the country.

Even today, people in many parts of Egypt lead lives that are very similar to the lives of people thousands of years ago. Some farmers till the rich soil by the Nile River as their **ancestors** did in ancient Egypt. Other Egyptians lead a more modern lifestyle in bustling cities like Alexandria and Cairo. Some people roam the arid desert while others cluster around its **fertile**, green **oases**. Wherever they live, Egypt's people are never far from the magnificent **monuments** that remind them of their country's glorious past.

(above) Police and security guards in Egypt use many different kinds of vehicles to suit their desert environment, including camels!

(right) A young Egyptian.

(right) A smiling woman's modest clothing reflects her religion and helps to shield her from the hot Egyptian sun.

(below) Egyptian youth often help their parents. This girl tends her parents' vegetable stand.

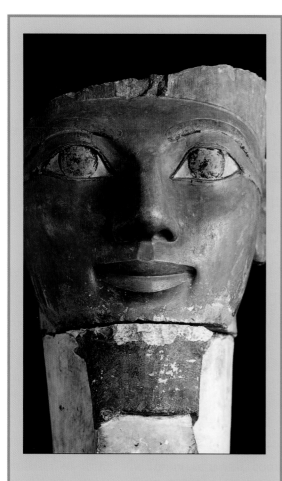

Hatshepsut
1478 B.C.–1458 B.C.

Hatshepsut was a powerful Pharaoh who sent troops into battle, sent traders out to the seas, and built beautiful temples. One thing makes this ruler very different from ancient Egypt's other Pharaohs – Hatshepsut was a woman! In the paintings and carvings on temples and tombs, she wears men's clothes, including the royal ceremonial beard. Despite her clothing, most Egyptians knew that they were being led by a woman: Hatshepsut means "foremost of the noble women."

Egypt's statues, **temples**, and **tombs** are reminders of the country's long and rich history. Now an independent nation, Egypt has been a kingdom, a powerful **empire**, and a **colony**.

Land of the Pharaohs

People have lived in the land of Egypt for thousands of years. Before 3100 B.C., Egypt was divided into Upper Egypt and Lower Egypt. In 3100 B.C., these two lands were united into a single kingdom, ruled by a king, or **Pharaoh**. The **reign** of the Pharaohs of ancient Egypt lasted for almost 3,000 years. Through the centuries, a great **civilization** grew up on the banks of the Nile. The ancient Egyptians had their own religion, rituals, writing system, art, and architecture.

Thutmose III
1458 B.C.–1436 B.C.

Thutmose III was Hatshepsut's stepson. He rose to power after she died. One of Egypt's greatest rulers, Thutmose III was a strong warrior. He conquered many countries and expanded the Egyptian Empire. The many riches that he collected during his wars made Egypt a very wealthy country.

Ruled by foreigners

By 1000 B.C., the rule of the Pharaohs was in decline. Over most of the next 3,000 years, non-Egyptians ruled Egypt. These rulers came from many places, including Libya, Greece, Rome, Arabia, Turkey, France, and England. In 332 B.C., the Greek emperor Alexander the Great **conquered** Egypt. He founded the city of Alexandria. The last of the Greek rulers, Queen Cleopatra, died in 30 B.C. Egypt then became a part of the Roman Empire, a territory that covered the Mediterranean region and beyond.

Akhenaton (Amenhotep IV)
1367 B.C.–1350 B.C.

Akhenaton was a rebel. He tried to change the religion of Egypt from the **worship** of many gods to the worship of one god. Many people did not agree with his beliefs. After Akhenaton's death, the rulers of Egypt turned back to the old religion and tried their best to erase all traces of his unpopular rule.

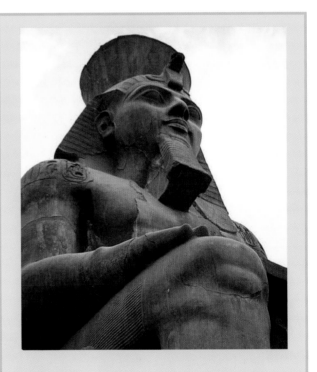

Ramses II
1290 B.C.–1224 B.C.

Ramses II would love his modern nickname – Ramses the Great. He was a clever politician who conquered many lands, but also made peace with his enemies. He built huge temples all over Egypt, including many to honor himself. Thousands of years ago, people were lucky if they lived to 40. Ramses ruled until his death, at 92 !

Cleopatra is one of the most famous women in history. She was a strong ruler known for her charm.

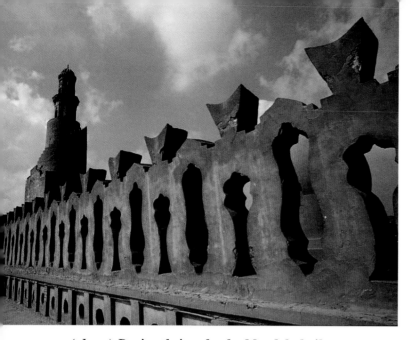

(above) *During their rule, the Mamluks built many beautiful* mosques, *or Islamic places of worship.*

(below) *The Arab ruler Ahmed Ibn Tulun had this mosque built in 879. It is the oldest in Cairo.*

The Arabs arrive

In 639 A.D., the Arabs invaded and Egypt became part of the great Arab Empire, which stretched from Spain to India. Most Egyptians adopted Islam, the religion of their rulers. They also began speaking Arabic, their rulers' language, instead of the ancient Egyptian language and the Greek language of Alexander. Power struggles continued in Egypt. Starting in 1250, Egypt was ruled by the Mamluks for 300 years. The Mamluk rulers were slaves who rose through the ranks of the Egyptian armies. Then, in 1517, the Turks invaded Egypt and made the country part of their empire until 1919.

In 1919, a woman makes a speech at a political rally protesting the British presence in Egypt.

From colony to kingdom

Even though Egypt was part of the Turkish Empire in the early 1900s, British power and influence grew in the country. At that time, many colonies and countries around the world were under the rule of the British Empire. During World War I (1914–1918), Britain declared Egypt a protected country under its rule and drove the Turks out. The country became independent in 1922, after Egyptians revolted and pressed for self-rule. King Fuad became the ruler but the real power in the country was still the British Empire, which tried to control Egypt. After King Fuad died in 1936, his son Farouk became the next king of Egypt.

Independence at last

In 1952, the Egyptians forced the British out of Egypt. Army officers took over power and forced the unpopular King Farouk to leave. For the first time in almost 20 centuries, Egypt was ruled completely by Egyptians. The country became the Arab Republic of Egypt, with both a president and a prime minister.

Gamal Abdel Nasser helped lead the revolt against King Farouk. This popular leader was the president of Egypt from 1956 until his death in 1970.

The people

Modern Egyptians are a mixture of all the peoples who lived and settled in Egypt during the past 5,000 years. They include people from Africa, Asia, the Middle East, and Europe. More than half of Egypt's people live in cities. The rest live in villages, oases, and the desert.

Egyptian Arabs

Arabs crossed the Red Sea and invaded Egypt 1,400 years ago, bringing their language, Arabic, and the religion of **Islam**. Egyptians today speak Arabic and most follow the religion of Islam. Followers of Islam are called Muslims. They worship *Allah*, the Arabic word for God, and follow the teachings of his **prophet** Muhammad. Other Egyptians are Christians called **Copts**. They follow the teachings of Jesus Christ, who they believe was God's son on earth.

Bedouins

For thousands of years, Bedouin tribes have traveled the deserts with their camels and goats. They are nomadic, meaning they are always searching for grazing land for their animals and fresh water for their families. They travel in large family groups. The leader of a group is called the *sheik*. Bedouins carry their homes with them wherever they go. They live in tents of goat and camel hair, which the women weave on their **looms**. Bedouins are known for their **hospitality**. Visitors are always invited to stay for three days and three nights, and to share stories with their hosts. Life is changing for the Bedouin. Many of them now live in houses and use trucks for transportation instead of camels.

(below) A young Bedouin waits patiently with his dog and camel.

(above) This young girl lives in Cairo, Egypt's capital city.

Nubians

Nubians have lived in southern Egypt since the time of the Pharaohs. They worked for the Pharaohs as highly trained soldiers, and as traders, carrying goods on their boats to and from other countries. They also used their boats to haul rock, and to transport villagers along the Nile River. Nubians used to farm the narrow strip of fertile land along the Nile. When the first **dam** was built at Aswan in 1902, its rising waters forced the Nubian people to move from the edge of the river to higher ground. This earth was **barren** and it was very difficult to grow crops. Many Nubian men went to the cities to find work. In the 1960s, there was more flooding when the Aswan High Dam was built. The Nubians were given fertile land farther north, which allowed many of the men to stay home and work the land.

(above) A Nubian family relaxes in their living room.

(below) In a tent on the Siwa Oasis, boys listen to friends playing music.

The Siwan people

The Siwan people live in the Siwa Oasis in the Western Desert. There, underground springs of water make it possible to grow crops, such as olives and dates. The Siwan are Muslims, but they speak the Siwan language, not Arabic. They have their own customs. One Siwan tradition is that on the evening before her wedding, the bride-to-be is led to a pool of water outside her village. There, an older woman bathes her. On the way home, the family of her husband-to-be meets her and gives her many gifts.

11

Village life

In ancient times, farmers did much of the work in the country. They helped build the Pharaoh's tombs and monuments. They also grew the food that fed workers. Today, most farmers, or *fellahin*, live where their ancestors did, in small villages along the Nile River.

Village homes

Newer villages have wide streets and houses that are made of sand bricks or cement blocks made in factories. Older villages have narrow streets and the houses are close together. Many houses are built of bricks made from the Nile's mud. When the bricks are dry and hard, all the people in a family build their own house. Sometimes, they trim the walls in blue because they believe that this color protects them from bad luck.

Most village houses have flat roofs, which Egyptians use as open-air bedrooms during the hottest times of the year.

Often, houses have a shady courtyard inthe middle. The refreshing air here cools down the rooms that surround the courtyard. Families relax in the courtyard and may also prepare their meals here instead of in the hot, stuffy kitchen.

Farming

Only seven percent of Egypt's land is good for growing crops and almost all of it is **irrigated**. The rest of the country is desert. On their plots of fertile land, *fellahin* plant beans, wheat, corn, and date palm trees. They also raise goats, ducks, and pigeons for their meat, and water buffalo for their milk. The water buffalo also plow the fields and work pumps that water the land. There are more people in Egypt than there used to be and there is less land for farming. Today, many people who live in villages work in cities or nearby towns. Some Egyptians even go to other countries to work.

Everyday chores

Everyone in a *fellahin* family has a job to do. The men till the fields or work in factories and shops in towns or cities. The women prepare the food, look after the house and the children, and care for the animals. Some husbands and wives work together in small family businesses. *Fellahin* children usually do their chores in the afternoon, when school is finished for the day. Young children help by herding the sheep and goats. Boys learn how to farm the land. Girls fetch water, milk the goats and water buffalo, and feed the chickens. When they are young, girls learn to carry loads on their heads. They start with loaves of bread. Then, after a lot of practice, they can walk and balance large clay jars of water on their heads without spilling a single drop!

(below) **A fellahin** *and his son bring animals to market where they will be slaughtered and their meat sold.*

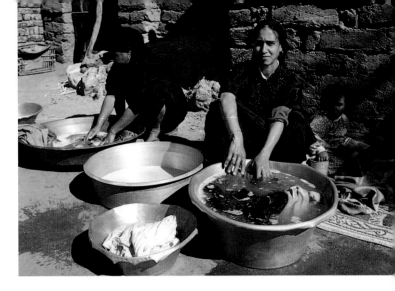

(above) **Village women do the laundry by hand.**

Family and friends

In an Egyptian village, people never have to worry about being alone. Uncles, aunts, cousins, and grandparents are always there to keep someone company or lend a helping hand. Often, the whole family works together and family members look after each other. If one person's crops are damaged, all the relatives share what they have. If an animal is badly injured and has to be killed, family members buy some of the meat. This way, *fellahin* have enough money to buy another animal.

City life

Egyptian cities are a mix of the old and the new, a place where the worlds of Africa, Europe, and Asia meet. These days, more Egyptians live in cities than ever before, especially in the busy cities of Alexandria and Cairo. Many people from the countryside have moved here, looking for work and a place to live. Cairo, the capital, grows by the day and its suburbs now stretch into the desert.

Merchants, locals, and tourists go about their business on a street in the old city of Cairo.

City homes

There is so little wood in Egypt that most city buildings are made of brick, cement, and steel, which are plentiful. The kinds of buildings vary, depending on the neighborhood. New neighborhoods have large houses or modern apartment buildings. In the older districts, large families squeeze into tiny apartments with balconies that overhang the twisting, narrow streets.

Tons of traffic

In Egyptian cities, the traffic never stops. Cars, buses, trucks, donkey carts, and crowds of people spill over the roads in every direction. Horns blare and loud music from radios and stereos fills the air. The cities are very crowded and it can take a long time to travel from one place to another, especially during rush hour.

Different neighborhoods

Egyptian cities are an exciting blend of neighborhoods and people. Some people follow ancient traditions and others lead modern lifestyles. Some people are rich and others are poor. Often, these people live side by side. Beautiful homes are built beside modest shacks. Lawyers, doctors, professors, and business people on their way to work pass families picking through garbage, looking for something to sell. **Shantytowns**, where people live in small huts, lie on the outskirts of cities. Nearby, air conditioners hum and satellite dishes speckle the roofs of modern houses and apartment buildings. Nearly everyone has a cell phone!

(left) Cars jam the roads of Cairo.

(below) People shop in the clothing section of a market.

(above) After hanging the wash, a woman watches the busy streets below.

Trying to narrow the gap

In Egypt, the gap between the rich and the poor seems to grow greater each year. Those people who could afford to go to school when they were younger learned how to read and write. Many of them have good jobs. Other people who had to work when they were younger never learned to read or write. Now, many of these people are poor and unemployed. The government and charitable agencies are working to change the situation and to make sure that everyone has access to a good education, health care, and nutritious food.

15

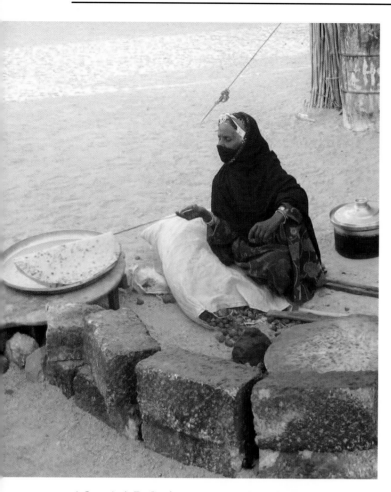

(above) A Bedouin woman cooks a flatbread on an outdoor stove.

(below) Desert storms can be dramatic! Some even kick up enough sand to be as tall as a pyramid.

Some desert dwellers, such as the Siwan people, live in towns and villages built on oases. Others, such as the Bedouin, are nomadic. They do not stay in one spot for very long. Wherever they go in the desert, they take their families, their animals, and their houses with them.

Reading the desert

In the Arabic language, Bedouin means "people of the desert." After thousands of years of moving all over the desert, the Bedouin know how to read the clues the desert leaves for them. Without this knowledge, they would not be able to survive in such a harsh land. When they see tracks in the sand, they know that travelers passed that way before, from which direction they came, what kinds of animals they had with them, and even the age of their camels. Shrubs and plants tell them when it last rained and how much rain fell. Bedouins navigate the seas of sand by the stars, by markers they left behind on other trips, and by familiar landmarks.

Desert homes

The traditional Bedouin home is a movable wool tent. The tent is divided in two by a woven curtain called a *ma'nad*. One part is called the *mag'ad*, or sitting place. This is where the men and most guests sit. The other part is the *maharama*, or place of the women. When the tribe moves, Bedouin women take down their family's home. They pack it on the camel's back and then put it up again in their new location. When it is very hot, Bedouins roll up the tent flaps so air can enter. In a sandstorm, the flaps are pinned down to keep the tent from blowing over.

(above) Bedouins camp at the foot of mountain cliffs.

Changing times

Life in the desert is slowly becoming more modern. Some Bedouins were given land by the government and now live in houses rather than tents. Instead of searching for water with their camels, they receive it by truck in 450-liter (100-gallon) barrels. Some drive pickup trucks instead of camels, and cell phones and televisions are common. Today, many Bedouins stand at the crossroads between two different worlds. Their way of life is changing, and nobody knows what the future will bring.

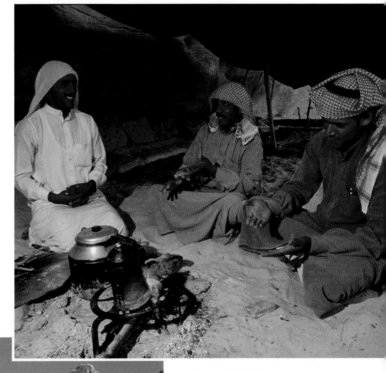

(above) Bedouin men chat as they wait for a pot of coffee to brew.

(left) A young Bedouin pulls water from a well to quench her camels' thirst.

17

Islam

More than 90 percent of all Egyptians are Muslims. There are two main groups of Muslims: the Sunni and the Shi'ites. Both groups use the same *Qur'an*, or **holy** book, follow Muhammad's teachings, and share many of the same beliefs. There is one big difference, though. When Muhammad died, some of his followers thought that they should vote for the next leader. The people who followed this leader became Sunni Muslims. Other followers thought that the next leader should be a member of Muhammad's family, and chose his son-in-law, Ali. These were Shi'ite Muslims. Most Muslims in Egypt are Sunni.

A way of life

For many Muslims, Islam is more than a religion. It is also a way of life. Muslims read *Allah's* words in the *Qu'ran*, which lays out many basic rules, such as what to eat and drink.

Muslims also read about Muhammad's sayings and deeds in *hadith*. Each *hadith* is a story about Muhammad that shows how wise he was and what a good life he led. By trying to follow Muhammad's example, Muslims believe they will come closer to leading a meaningful life.

The Five Pillars of Islam

There are five things that all religious Muslims must try to do and they are called the pillars of the **faith**. First, they must declare their faith in front of other people. Second, they must pray to *Allah* five times every day: at daybreak, noon, afternoon, sunset, and evening. Every year, they must give a certain amount of money to people in need. They must **fast** from dawn to sunset every day during the holy month of Ramadan. Finally, those who can, make a **pilgrimage** to Mecca, the holy city in the country of Saudi Arabia where Muhammad was born. This pilgrimage is called a *hajj*.

Muslim girls study the Qur'an with the help of a teacher.

Ramadan

Ramadan is the ninth and holiest month of the Islamic year. During Ramadan, religious Muslims do not eat or drink anything from sunrise to sunset. Children up to the age of twelve and pregnant women do not usually fast. Muslims believe fasting teaches them **self-discipline** and reminds them of all the good things that *Allah* has given them. When the sun goes down, people break their fast with a few dates or a glass of water. Then, they eat a big meal called *iftar*. After *iftar*, large crowds jam the streets to listen to storytellers and musicians. Stores and restaurants stay open late, and people visit family and friends.

Eid al-Fitr

Ramadan ends with a joyful celebration called Eid al-Fitr. Eid lasts for three days and is a public holiday. Traditionally, everyone gets new clothes. Houses are filled with flowers and are often decorated with banners. Children, especially, look forward to Eid because they receive toys and candy. Families visit and bring gifts to share a midday feast together.

(top) So many people have come to the mosque, a Muslim place of worship, that a whole crowd must pray outside.

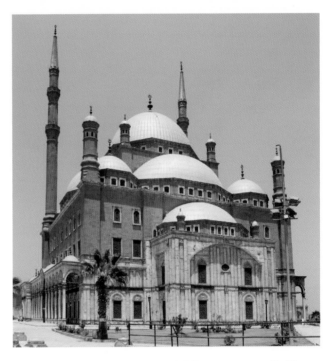

(above) Cairo's Muhammad Ali mosque was built in the 1800s with alabaster domes.

Radical Islam

Egypt has endured several terrorist attacks by members of **Islamic fundamentalist** groups who want to bring down the government and install one that is more religious and observant. In 1997, terrorists killed 68 people in an attack on the tourist site of Luxor. The terrorists do not represent the views of most Egyptian Muslims.

Festivals

The Egyptian year is crammed with festivals. Some celebrate the ancient **heritage** of the land, others celebrate the religion of the people who live there, and still others celebrate important people and special times of the year.

Moulids

Moulids, or festivals of religious figures, are huge, popular gatherings that Muslims and Christians look forward to every year. Each town, village, and city has its own moulid. A moulid may last from two days to two weeks. People crowd into the streets to listen to musicians and storytellers, and to watch the religious dancers known as **dervishes**. Adults visit each other, while children enjoy fun-filled carnivals with all kinds of rides and games.

Dervishes are religious dancers famous for their high-paced, whirling dance.

People watch dazzling displays of lights or take part in long, winding parades. The most impressive parade takes place in Cairo for the Moulid el-Nabi. This festival honors the birthday of the Muslim prophet Muhammad.

Sham el-Nessim

The festival of Sham el-Nessim goes all the way back to the time of the Pharaohs. When families gather in April for this holiday, that is the sign that spring has come again to Egypt. Sham el-Nessim means "sniffing of the breeze." That is exactly what Egyptians do, as they enjoy an outdoor meal in a park or by the banks of the Nile River. Their picnic includes special foods, which they believe prevent disease, such as salt fish, called *fesikh*, and green onions. Children dye eggs many different colors to represent the new life that comes with spring.

This colossus, or huge statue, of Ramses II is so big that a person could sit comfortably in one of its ears!

Happy birthday, Ramses II!

Twice a year, a festival is held at Aswan, in the south of Egypt, to honor the great Pharaoh, Ramses II. February 21 is his birthday and October 21 is his **coronation**, the day he was crowned king. In Ramses' famous temple, Abu Simbel, four statues sit in a deep, dark room. On these two days, a ray of sun used to shine all the way through the temple and onto the faces of three of the four statues. During Ramses II's time, these were very special days. Then in the 1960s, when the Aswan High Dam was built, Abu Simbel was moved to save it from the rising waters of the Nile. This massive project involved moving the entire temple and positioning it at the same angle. The sun still shines on the statues twice a year, but one day later than before. Now every year on February 22 and October 22, people celebrate Ramses II's birthday and coronation at the reconstructed temple on higher ground.

(above) Sun shines on the huge statues of Ramses II inside Abu Simbel.

Family events

People in Egypt mark all of life's events, from birth to death, with special ceremonies. These ceremonies always involve the family and often the community, too.

The birth blessing

Seven days after a baby is born, there is a ceremony called *sebou* (pronounced "se-bo-oo"), which means "the seventh day." The baby is placed on the floor and the mother carefully steps over her infant seven times. Grains, such as wheat and rice, are sprinkled to the north, south, east, and west. Everyone invited to the *sebou* makes a lot of noise so that when the baby grows up, he or she will not be startled by loud sounds. Then, all the guests enjoy sweets and strong coffee.

Celebrating marriage

In Egypt, marriages are joyful celebrations that join two families, as well as two people. Muslims are usually married at home. The *imam*, or priest, comes to the bride's home and reads verses from the *Qur'an*. After the readings, a marriage **contract** is signed. Then, the wedding celebrations begin. Some celebrations take place outside, while others take place in a hotel. The bride is brought into the hall, surrounded by dancers, singers, and tambourine players. Trumpets sound, the event is photographed and filmed, and hundreds of guests enjoy the party.

(above) Children represent the future of the Egyptian people.

(below) An entire village joins a traditional wedding procession along the banks of the Nile. The bride is riding on the back of a camel, inside a covered canopy.

Funeral farewells

Like everything else in Egypt, a person's death is part of family and community life. Christian funerals are held in the church and the person who died is buried in a plain wooden coffin. When a Muslim dies, family members follow Islamic tradition and wash the body with love and care, and then wrap it in white cloth. After the washing of the body, male relatives and friends lead a procession to the mosque or the cemetery, taking turns carrying the body. It is considered a good deed to join the procession, even if you do not know the person who died.

At the mosque or grave, the *imam* recites prayers aloud, friends and family say silent prayers, and the person is buried. On the evening of the burial, some wealthy families block off the street where the person lived and set up a tent for the **mourners**. Sometimes, they also hire a professional Qur'an reader, called a *maqri*. For several evenings after the burial, the Qur'an is read in the home of the person who died and food is given to the poor.

(above) Two mourners sit among the graves in a Muslim graveyard.

(above) Workers set up a funeral tent.

Sports and pastimes

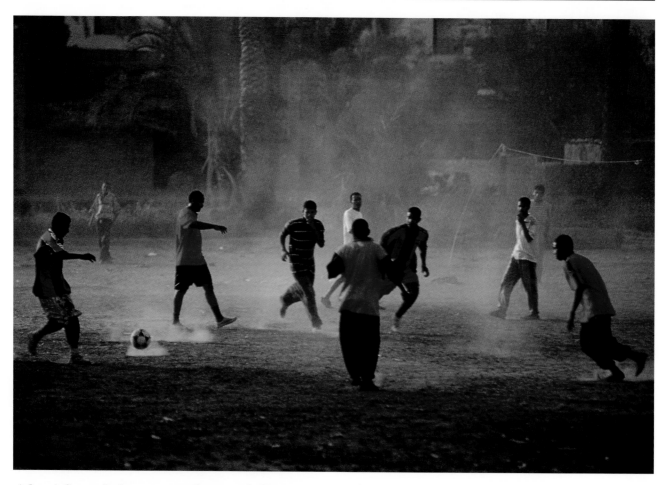

(above) Soccer is the most popular sport in Egypt.

(below) A family enjoys drinks in a Cairo tearoom.

Like children all over the world, Egyptian children love to play games such as hide-and-seek, piggyback, and *seegha*, a game similar to marbles that is played with pebbles. Some of these games can be traced back to the time of ancient Egypt. Others are more recent.

Get that ball!

Egypt is crazy about soccer. When an important match is played in Cairo, almost every seat at the stadium is taken. People crowd around radios and televisions in their homes and in cafés to follow every move and every goal. It is not only adults who love soccer. Children all over the country play soccer in streets and fields. If they do not have a soccer ball, they make one out of old socks tied together!

Cafés, conversation, and checkers

Although many people in Egypt work hard, they also know how to relax and enjoy themselves. The cities and towns are full of cafés where men gather for long hours to chat, play a game of checkers, and drink a cup of strong coffee or hot tea. They catch up on the latest news or play backgammon, chess, dominoes, or cards. In the evening, some cafés show television shows and videos from Egypt, India, or the United States. In Cairo alone, there are 5,000 cafés to choose from. People also like to gather around *asiir* or juice stands. Here, they can sip juice made from sugar cane, limes, tangerines, and guavas.

The Game of Two Kingdoms

When Egypt was divided into two kingdoms, Upper Egypt was known as the white kingdom and Lower Egypt was known as the red kingdom. After the two kingdoms were united, the Pharaoh wore a double crown of both colors. Today, children sometimes play the Game of Two Kingdoms. Seven bricks are stacked in a pile. Children then divide into two teams, the white team for Upper Egypt and the red team for Lower Egypt. Each team takes turns knocking down the pile with a ball. The first team to demolish the pile wins the game.

(left) A boy rides a camel through a crowd. Camel racing is a popular sport in Egypt.

(below) A couple of boys row their handmade boats down the Nile.

There are millions of children under the age of fifteen in Egypt, and not enough schools or teachers. Often, children have to go to school in two shifts, morning and afternoon. There may be as many as 45 or 50 students in one classroom. All children are supposed to attend school until the end of junior high. Many continue through high school and university, too. Education is free in the public school system, although some parents pay to send their children to private school.

Zaineb goes to school

It is 7 a.m. on a Tuesday morning in Cairo. Zaineb, who is eleven years old, and Jabir, her brother who just turned nine, are getting ready for school. Zaineb is already sitting at the table, dipping her bits of *aysh*, or bread, into a plate of *fuul*. She smacks her lips over the last little bit of the bean paste and calls to her brother, "Jabir, are we going to see you today or tomorrow? Did you forget that school starts at 7:45?"

While Jabir munches his breakfast, Zaineb gathers her books for the day's classes. She is in Grade 5 and is studying Arabic, English, history, geography, science, and mathematics. She checks to make sure that she has her homework. "*Mama*, we're leaving now." Zaineb calls to her mother, who comes out into the hall to give each child a quick hug. "Remember to hurry home. Geda is going to make your favorite dish today. I'll be late getting home from work," Mama says. Zaineb is excited. She loves her grandmother and she loves her grandmother's cooking, too.

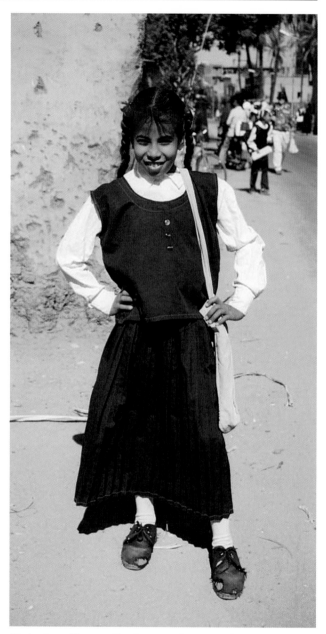

Zaineb walks to school every day wearing her navy blue school uniform.

Zaineb and Jabir's school is only three blocks from their apartment, so they walk back and forth together every morning and afternoon. They are lucky to live that close. Zaineb's best friend, Laila, has to come on the school bus every day. No matter how early the bus starts out, it always gets caught in a traffic jam!

(below) On their way home, Zaineb and her classmates buy roasted nuts from a street vendor.

(above) Zaineb loves basketball, but she rarely has a chance to play because the older students always seem to be on the court.

At 7:45, the school bell rings. All the children salute the flag, sing the national anthem, and do some exercises in the schoolyard. Then, they file into the school. Each of Zaineb's classes lasts 45 minutes. This year, her favorite subject is geography.

In the middle of the morning, there is a recess break. After eating a sandwich, Zaineb plays hopscotch and skipping games with her friends. By 2:30, the day's classes are over, and Zaineb and her friends pour out of the school. When they get home, they will have a late lunch, the biggest meal of the day.

As they reach home, Zaineb and Jabir see geda waiting at the door to greet them. Delicious aromas waft in from the kitchen. Once the meal is over and baba, their dad, has returned from praying at the mosque, Zaineb and Jabir spend a bit more time with geda and baba. Then, it is time for homework. Every night, Zaineb has a lot of assignments to do. If she is lucky, she finishes early enough to watch some television or go for an evening stroll with her family before she goes to bed.

27

Clothes

In Egypt, people dress in a mix of traditional and modern styles. Some Egyptians wear traditional clothes that keep them cool in the hot climate. Other people wear clothing that follows the rules of their religion. When they are in public, very religious Muslims cover their heads and their bodies from their wrists to their ankles. Some women also wear a veil across their face. This is part of following *hijab*, a code that tells Muslims to act and dress **modestly**.

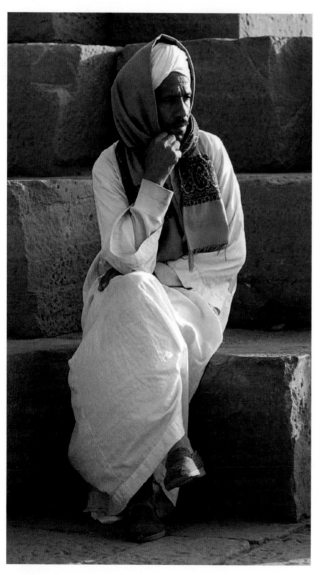

A man dressed in traditional clothing sits on the blocks of an ancient monument.

Country clothing

A *fellahin* woman who is married usually puts on a black coatdress over her brightly colored housedress when she leaves her home. She does this to be modest in public. She covers her hair with a long scarf and wears all her jewelry. Her parents gave her silver and gold necklaces, bracelets, and anklets when she got married. This jewelry is her wealth, in case her husband dies or divorces her. *Fellahin* men wear loose cotton robes called *galabiyyahs*. Some men also cover their heads with scarves wound like a *turban*. On colder days, *fellahin* men wear woolen *galabiyyahs* and jackets. Many *fellahin* still wear their traditional clothes after they move to the city.

City style

Many people wear modern clothes, such as pants, shirts, dresses, and jackets. That is especially true for people who work in offices. When they arrive home from work, many men change out of their modern clothes into a comfortable *galabiyyah*. Others relax in blue jeans and running shoes.

Desert dress

Bedouins dress for the heat of the desert. The men keep cool by wearing layers of loose robes. To prevent heat stroke and to protect their face from sun and sand, they wind a cloth, or *koffiiya*, around their head and neck. Bedouin women wear long black dresses. Married women wrap *asabas*, or black head cloths with colored stitches, around their foreheads. Then, they cover their faces with black veils.

(above) In Egypt, some women wear headscarves, while others choose not to.

(right) On special occasions, Bedouin women wear black robes with intricate stitching and beadwork.

(below) Many Egyptians wear modern but modest jeans and shirts.

Food

Throughout the centuries, as people from different countries settled in Egypt, they added new ingredients and flavors to Egyptian cooking. Egyptian cooks created tasty dishes by changing Greek, Syrian, Turkish, and Lebanese recipes to fit Egyptian tastes. In every village, town, and city, street vendors cook and sell all kinds of food to people passing by. There is always a delicious snack to try!

Bread and beans

Chances are that, if you lived in Egypt, you would eat *fuul* for breakfast. You might even eat it for lunch or dinner, too. *Fuul* is Egypt's national dish. It is made with stewed beans, oil, lemon, spices, and sometimes, tomatoes. Most people eat *fuul* with bread or *aysh*. Egyptian bread can be hard and flat, or soft with a pocket. You can stuff fillings like vegetables and sauces inside the pocket to make a sandwich. In some villages, all the women bake bread together. That way, they get to catch up on the latest news while they prepare food for their families.

Pigeon houses and tasty dishes

Fellahin use mud to build tall pigeon houses called **dovecotes**. They raise pigeons, or *hammams*, for their meat. The pigeons are stuffed with rice and then roasted. This dish is a special treat because many Egyptians cannot afford to eat meat very often.

(above) **Fuul** *is served in a common bowl and* **aysh** *is used to scoop it up.*

(opposite) A family eats breakfast together.

Halal meat

Chicken, lamb, and beef are popular foods in Egypt. Many Egyptians do not eat pork because their religion, Islam, forbids it. Muslims eat only *halal*, or lawful foods, that are permitted by the *Qur'an*. They also kill and prepare their food according to the instructions in the *Qur'an*.

Mealtimes

In Egypt, the main meal is usually eaten in the middle of the day. Egyptians often have a nap after this meal, especially during the hotter summer months. *Fellahin* usually have vegetables cooked in butter, tomatoes, and rice for their main meal. They eat the lighter evening meal long after the sun goes down. Some Egyptians use knives and forks when they eat, but *fellahin* use traditional methods and scoop up their food with bread instead of a fork.

*(below) A **halal** butcher prepares meat at an open-air market. He follows the Qur'an's instructions for killing and preparing the meat.*

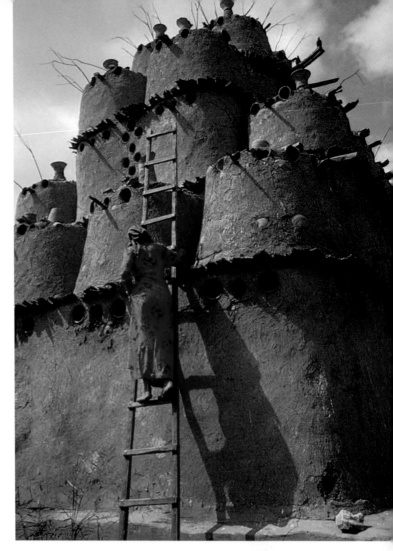

(above) A woman perches on a ladder to collect pigeons' eggs from a huge dovecote.

A recipe for sweet *koshaf*

Here is an Egyptian recipe for a delicious dessert to satisfy your sweet tooth.

1 cup (250 mL) dried prunes
1 cup (250 mL) dried apricots
1 cup (250 mL) dried figs, halved
1 1/2 cups (375 mL) raisins
1 cup (250 mL) sugar (more if you like it sweeter)
2 1/2 cups (625 mL) boiling water

Put all the fruit in a container. Sprinkle the sugar over the fruit and pour the boiling water on top. Cover the container. When the fruit cools down, put the container in the refrigerator. *Koshaf* is most delicious when the fruit is left overnight or for several hours before eating.

31

Glossary

ancestor A person from whom one is descended

barren Unable to produce crops or vegetation

capital A city where the government of a state or country is located

civilization A society with a well established culture that has existed for a long period of time

colony An area controlled by a distant country

conquer To gain control over a land by using force

contract An agreement between two or more people

Copts Christians from the Church of Egypt

coronation A ceremony to crown a leader

dam A wall built across a river to hold back water

dervish A member of a Muslim group who has taken a vow of poverty and expresses spirituality through dance

dovecote A structure with nesting holes for pigeons

empire A group of countries under one ruler or government

faith Religious belief

fast To stop eating food or certain kinds of food for religious or health reasons

fertile Able to produce abundant crops or vegetation

heritage Customs, objects, and achievements handed down from earlier generations

holy Having special religious importance

hospitality A welcoming and friendly attitude toward visitors

imam A Muslim religious leader

irrigated Supplied with water by artificial means

Islam The religion of Muslims

Islamic fundamentalist Someone who has an extreme interpretation of the Islamic religion

loom A device used to weave strands of thread together to produce cloth

modestly In a manner that does not seek attention

monument A structure built to remember a person or event

mosque A Muslim place of worship

mourner A person showing grief over a death

oasis An area in a desert where plants grow because there is water. The plural of oasis is oases

Pharaoh A ruler of ancient Egypt

pilgrimage A religious journey to a special place

prophet A person who is believed to speak on behalf of God

reign A royal ruler's period of time in power

self-discipline The ability to control one's feelings and actions

shantytown A poor area of a city with many makeshift houses or shacks

temple A building used for religious services

tomb A chamber or room for burying the dead

worship To honor or respect a god

 # Index